DECLARATION
•

I hereby declare that
all the paper produced
by Cartiere del Garda S.p.A.
in its Riva del Garda mill
is manufactured completely
<u>Acid-free and Wood-free</u>

Alois Lueftinger

Dr. Alois Lueftinger
Managing Director and General Manager
Cartiere del Garda S.p.A.

GREEN WORLD

FERNS

Written by
Theresa Greenaway

STECK-VAUGHN
LIBRARY
A Division of Steck-Vaughn Company

Austin, Texas

Editor: Wendy Madgwick
Designer: Jane Hunt
Illustrators: Wendy and Clifford Meadway

Notes to Reader
There are some words in this book that are printed in **bold** type.
A brief explanation of these words is given in the glossary on p. 44.

All living things are given two Latin names when first classified by a
scientist. Some of them also have a common name, for example, water
clover, *Marsilea quadrifolia*. In this book, the common name is used
where possible, but the scientific name is given when first mentioned.

Library of Congress Cataloging-in-Publication Data

Greenaway, Theresa, 1947-
Ferns / written by Theresa Greenaway.
p. cm. – (The Green world)
Includes bibliographical references and index.
Summary: Examines the characteristics, life cycle, and
natural environment of various types of ferns and discusses
their uses as natural medicines and food.
ISBN 0-8114-2735-8
1. Ferns – Juvenile literature. [1. Ferns.] I. Title. II. Series.
QK522.5.G74 1991
587'.3 – dc20   91-14935
CIP   AC

Color separations by Chroma Graphics, Singapore
Printed and bound by L.E.G.O., Vicenza, Italy
1 2 3 4 5 6 7 8 9 0 LE 96 95 94 93 92

Photographic credits
t = top, b = bottom, l = left, r = right
Cover: Bruce Coleman; page 10 Bruce Coleman/H. Reinhard;
page 13 Bruce Coleman/A. Compost; page 14 C.N. Page; page 15 Frank
Lane/G. Dickson; page 17 Frank Greenaway; page 19 United States
Travel and Tourism Agency; page 21 Bruce Coleman/M. Freeman;
page 23*t* Bruce Coleman/E. Pott; page 23*b* Frank Lane/K.G. Preston;
page 27 Bruce Coleman/Eckart Pott; page 28 Frank Lane/Premaphotos
Wildlife; page 30*l* Frank Lane/A.R. Hamblin; page 30*r* Frank Lane/K.G.
Preston-Mafham; page 31 Frank Lane/L. Batten; page 32 Frank
Lane/M.J. Thomas; page 33*t* Frank Lane/J. Watkins;
page 33*b* Bruce Coleman/J. Cowan; page 34 J. Allan Cash;
page 37 Frank Lane/K.G. Preston-Mafham;
page 42 Bruce Coleman/H. Reinhard.

CONTENTS

Green World.................................... 6

Ferns... 8

All Sizes and Shapes........................ 10

Tropical Ferns................................ 12

Mountain Ferns.............................. 14

Ferns of Wet Places 16

Woodland Ferns............................. 18

The Fern Plant 20

The Fern Frond 22

Other Pteridophytes........................ 24

Life Cycles 26

Spreading Spores 28

How Ferns Survive 30

Bracken...................................... 32

Threatened Habitats........................ 34

New "Homes" 36

Plants That Made Coal...................... 38

The Greenhouse Effect..................... 40

Uses of Ferns................................ 42

Glossary 44

Further Reading............................. 44

Ferns in This Book 45

Index... 46

GREEN WORLD

This tree shows the different groups of plants that are found in the world. It does not show how they developed or their relationship with each other.

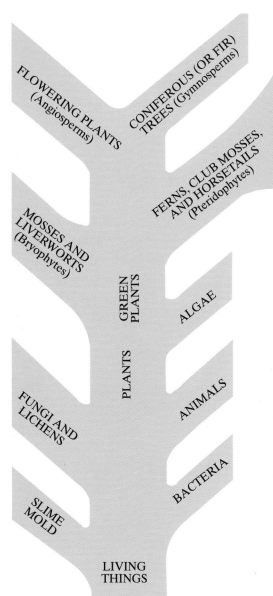

FLOWERING PLANTS (Angiosperms)

CONIFEROUS (OR FIR) TREES (Gymnosperms)

FERNS, CLUB MOSSES, AND HORSETAILS (Pteridophytes)

MOSSES AND LIVERWORTS (Bryophytes)

GREEN PLANTS

ALGAE

PLANTS

ANIMALS

FUNGI AND LICHENS

BACTERIA

SLIME MOLD

LIVING THINGS

Group 1: Fork ferns
- No roots
- Shoots grow from a creeping underground stem
- Scale or "false" leaves only

Group 2: Club mosses
- Simple leaves in whorls or spirals, one vein
- All living kinds are small, but many extinct kinds were large trees

Group 3: Horsetails
- Shoots upright and stiff, reinforced with silica
- Branches in whorls
- Leaves are whorled scale leaves
- Spores develop in a conelike strobilus

Group 4: True ferns
Ophioglossales
- Small plants, simple in structure
- Fronds not coiled when young
- Spore cases with thick, many-layered wall

Marattiales
- Often large plants with huge fronds
- Stipes fleshy, wilting quickly in drought
- Spore cases with thick, many-layered wall

Filicales
- Largest and very variable group
- Spore cases with thin, single-layered wall

The land area of the world is divided into ten main zones depending on the types of plants that grow there. Ferns and other pteridophytes are found in damp areas throughout the world.

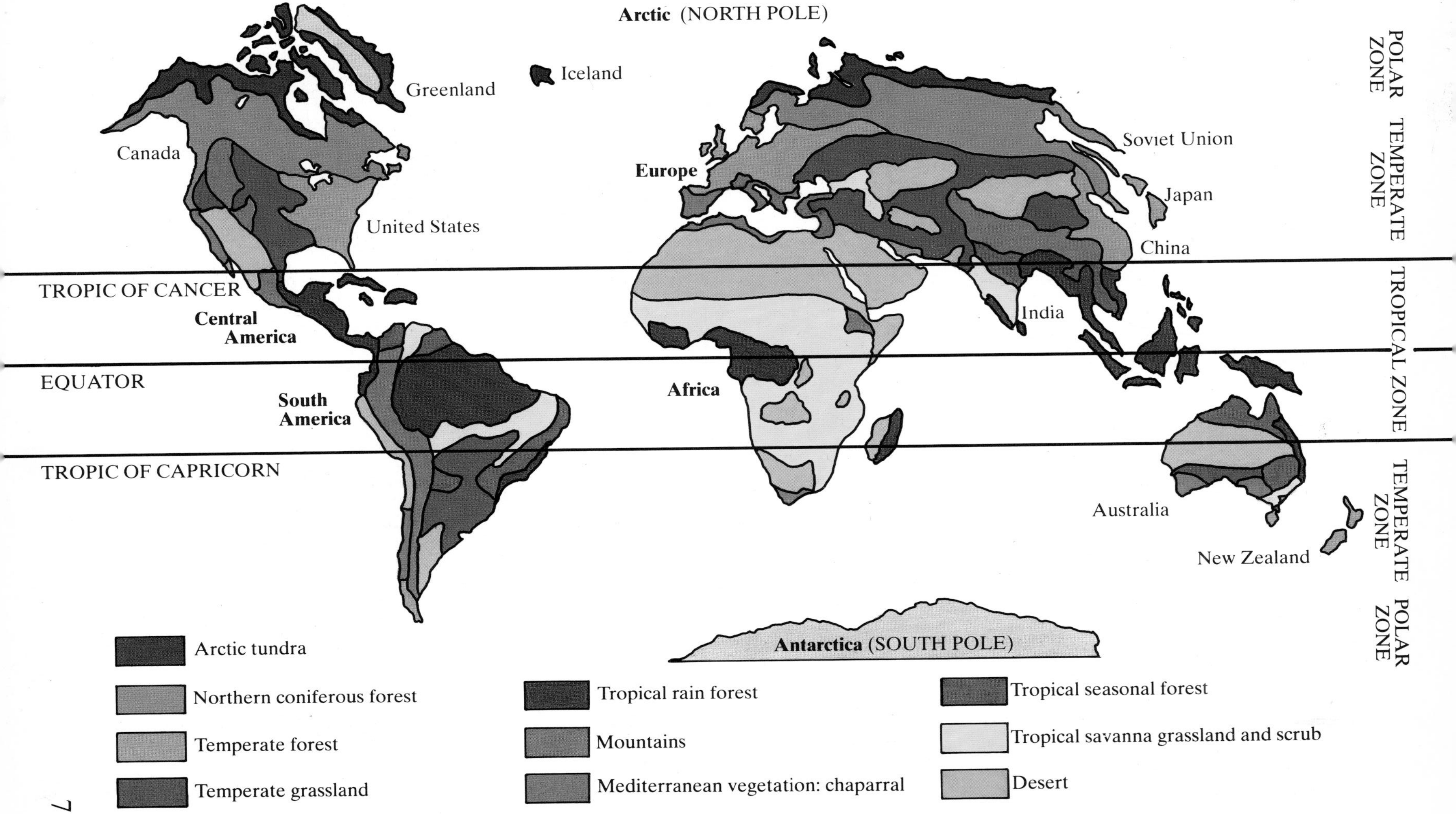

POLAR ZONE   TEMPERATE ZONE   TROPICAL ZONE   TEMPERATE ZONE   POLAR ZONE

Arctic (NORTH POLE)

Soviet Union
Japan
China
India
Iceland
Greenland
United States
Canada
Europe
Africa
New Zealand
Australia
Central America
South America

Antarctica (SOUTH POLE)

TROPIC OF CANCER
EQUATOR
TROPIC OF CAPRICORN

Arctic tundra
Northern coniferous forest
Temperate forest
Temperate grassland

Tropical rain forest
Mountains
Mediterranean vegetation: chaparral

Tropical seasonal forest
Tropical savanna grassland and scrub
Desert

7

FERNS

Ferns and their relations are plants that do not have flowers, and instead of seeds they have **spores**. They are the most advanced of all the seedless plants because they are the only nonflowering plants that have special conducting, or vascular, strands in their stems. The **xylem** carries water up the plant and the **phloem** carries food (see p. 21). The other spore-bearers, algae, fungi, lichens, mosses, and liverworts, do not have these strands. Ferns have two stages in their life cycle: a large **sporophyte**, the fern plant, and a tiny, much-reduced **gametophyte**, the **prothallus** (see p. 26).

Like all green plants, ferns contain the green pigment **chlorophyll**. The energy in sunlight activates the chlorophyll, so that carbon dioxide gas from the air is combined with water to make simple sugars and oxygen. These sugars can then be made into other food for the plant. This is the vitally important process called **photosynthesis**.

Ferns and their relatives

Ferns and their close relations, the fork ferns, club mosses, quillworts, and horsetails, are all classed in a group that botanists (people who study plants) call **pteridophytes**. Different kinds of pteridophytes can be found in most parts of the world except deserts and very cold regions. However, most of the 12,000 or so species are found in tropical and subtropical regions. Although quite a few species live in fresh water, only the fern *Acrostichum aureum* is found in salty water, in tropical mangrove swamps.

Fork ferns (*Psilotum* species) are simple pteridophytes similar to the earliest known fossils of vascular plants, which lived about 400 million years ago. There are only four species that grow in the tropics and subtropics.

Quillworts live in either marshy ground or freshwater lakes. There are about 70 species and they all have long, narrow leaves. They often look like a tuft of grass.

Ferns

Ferns are the largest group of the pteridophytes, containing about 10,400 species. Ferns are very varied in shape and size.

Lady ferns (*Athyrium*) are "typical" ferns growing in woods and along fence lines.

Shoestring ferns (*Vittaria*) grow on rocks and trees in tropical rain forests.

- Ferns belong to the group pteridophytes.
- They are green plants and make their food by photosynthesis.
- They have two stages in their life cycle. The main stage is the sporophyte (the fern plant). The gametophyte stage is a tiny and short-lived prothallus.
- They contain xylem and phloem vessels in their stems.

The largest ferns are the tree ferns, many of which are over 45 feet tall.

Club mosses contain the true club mosses (*Lycopodium* species) and the spikemosses (*Selaginella* species). There are about 1,100 kinds of these fairly small plants. Most prefer moist places or **habitats**; though a few spikemosses are found in quite dry places.

Horsetails are mostly medium to large plants that often grow in very noticeable patches. They have stiff, upright stems with tiny brown or colorless leaves. Both branches and leaves grow in whorls. They grow in the tropics and colder parts of temperate regions.

ALL SIZES AND SHAPES

Fern leaves are called fronds. Spores develop on the undersides of the fronds or on specially modified fronds. Botanists have put the ferns into groups, or families, according to the appearance of the leaves and the arrangement of the spore-bearing parts. There are about 20 families! The selection shown here will give you some idea of the different kinds of fern and the different places they are found.

Tree ferns

There are about 350 kinds of tree fern, all found in the tropics and the subtropical part of the southern hemisphere – New Zealand, Australia, Africa, and South America. Most, like the Australian tree fern (see below), are only about 8 feet tall. The black tree fern (*Cyathea medullaris*) of New Zealand can grow to 65 feet with a crown 45 feet across!

Adder's tongue ferns

These are found in tropical and temperate regions. Most have a simple frond with a spike that produces spores growing from its base. Adder's tongue (*Ophioglossum vulgatum*, see above) grows in North America, Europe, Asia, and North Africa in damp grassland and marshy places.

Royal ferns

This is a small family found on wet, peaty soils in most parts of the world except Australia. The young shoots are fuzzy with thick, matted hairs. Spores are produced on special parts of the frond. The royal fern *Osmunda regalis* (see above) is found in North and South America, Europe, Asia, and Africa.

Filmy ferns

This is a large family of about 650 species. Their fronds are so thin and delicate that they dry out very quickly. They live in moist, shady places such as tropical forests. A few, such as Wilson's filmy fern, (*Hymenophyllum wilsonii*, see above) are found farther north in wet, misty coastal areas.

Polypody ferns

Different species of these ferns grow all over the world. The common polypody (*Polypodium vulgare*, see above) grows in North America, Europe, Asia, and South Africa. It is often called the wall fern because it sprouts from crevices in walls. It also grows on tree trunks and the ground.

Marsilea ferns

These strange ferns have fronds that look just like four-leaved clovers. They grow in marshy places in warm and tropical parts of the world, especially where there is often flooding. Water clover (*Marsilea quadrifolia*, see above) is found in North America, southern Europe, China, and Japan.

Maidenhair ferns

This is a large group of very beautiful ferns. The fragile fronds often have fine black stems and many tiny leaflets. They are most abundant in warm, frost-free climates, and only the common maidenhair (*Adiantum capillus-veneris*, see above) grows as far north as Ireland and coastal west Britain.

TROPICAL FERNS

The idea that a tropical rain forest has a lush undergrowth of dense greenery is not really accurate. Only in clearings and along the edges of the forest beside streams and roads is there enough light at ground level for flowering plants and ferns to flourish. Deep in the dark, gloomy interior, the thick canopy of evergreen leaves screens out almost all the sunlight. Many smaller, nonwoody plants have moved upward to the light and live as **epiphytes** on the branches, leaves, and twigs of the forest giants, some 90 feet above ground level.

This treetop garden includes some weird and wonderful ferns. A few of these are familiar to people far away from their native forests. They are sold worldwide as potted plants for homes, conservatories, and greenhouses.

Stag's horn ferns

The stag's horn ferns (*Platycerium* species, see below) are found in all tropical rain forests. Each area has its own particular kind. They are an easily recognized group, with two very different sorts of frond. At the base of the plant, some fronds grow into flat, platelike brackets that clasp the tree trunk. The rest grow outward to make a mass of hanging fronds, each resembling an antler. Dead leaves, debris, and water collect behind the flat fronds, so each fern has its own supply of nutrients.

The South American stag's horn (*P. andinum*) has hanging fronds that are divided into narrow lobes.

The elkhorn fern (*P. bifurcatum*) is a large fern from tropical Australia and Indonesia.

The elephant's ear fern (*P. elephantotis*) has wavy-edged bracket fronds and the hanging fronds are large and undivided, just like green elephant's ears.

Ferns as epiphytes

The bird's nest fern (*Asplenium nidus*, see right) has a bright green rosette of fronds. Water trickles down each leaf and collects at the base of the plant, where it can be taken up by the roots. The common tassel fern (*Lycopodium phlegmaria*) is an epiphytic club moss with hanging, branched stems.

Scramblers, climbers, and giants

Climbing ferns have their roots in the moist leaf mold of the shady forest floor, and then scramble up taller trees to reach the light. They have two kinds of fronds quite different in appearance. The lowest leaves of *Lygodium* have a thin, broad shape to make the most of any available light. Farther up, at the top of the fern, a second spore-bearing type of frond is found.

The Malaysian climbing fern *Lygodium* can reach up to 30 feet.

The giant fern (*Angiopteris evecta*) has enormous curving fronds between 10 and 20 feet long.

The umbrella fern (*Gleichenia microphyllum*), a scrambling tropical fern, has fronds up to 10 feet long.

MOUNTAIN FERNS

The Earth's crust is made up of layers of many kinds of rocks. Folds, cracks, volcanic activity, and erosion all mean that the layers, or seams, are quite often mixed up. Even very hard rocks release tiny amounts of the minerals they contain into the groundwater. Rocks and soils are described as being "acidic" or "basic." For example, granite and sandstone are acidic rocks; limestone and chalk are basic. Some ferns are equally successful on both kinds of soil. Others grow best on one or the other, and a few are restricted to just one kind. For instance, green spleenwort (*Asplenium viride*) will only grow on limestone rocks, and parsley fern (*Cryptogramma crispa*) is limited to acid areas.

Wind and rain carry the tiny spores of ferns and mosses onto the rocks. The damp conditions, especially on north-facing slopes, are ideal for their successful **germination** and the growth of the delicate prothalli (see p. 26). The fine fern roots grow into the tiniest of cracks in the rocks, securing the plant firmly even on steep-sided gullies. Ferns can grow well in very small pockets of soil, and the water trickling down from above provides them with additional nutrients.

All over the world!
The brittle bladder fern (*Cystopteris fragilis*, see right) is the most widespread fern in the world. It grows as far north as Greenland, on northern mountains of North America, Europe, Asia, and on high mountain slopes of tropical mountains and as far south as Kerguelen Island, in the Southern Ocean off Antarctica.

Ferns of northern mountains

The slopes of mountain ranges in North America, Europe, and Asia have very similar communities of pteridophytes, especially on the high ledges and cliffs above the treeline. Many species are found on all three continents.

Diphasiastrum alpinum

moonwort (*Botrychium lunaria*)

Asplenium viride

Cryptogramma crispa

holly fern (*Polystichum lonchitis*)

Athyrium distentifolium

Ferns of southern mountains

The mountains of South America, New Zealand, and southeast Australia also have ferns not found north of the equator. Some of these are very hardy. The prickly shield fern (*Polystichum vestitum*) of New Zealand has tough, prickly fronds that survive frost and snow. The alpine water fern (*Blechnum penna-marina*, see left) grows on all southern mountains. It is one of the very few plants able to grow on islands in the subantarctic. Its shorter, more compact fronds help it survive the very severe weather on these islands.

FERNS OF WET PLACES

Pteridophytes are found in freshwater lakes, pools, and marshes all over the world. Wetlands are important because they provide food and living quarters for a wide variety of birds and other animals, including many invertebrates (animals without backbones).

Floating ferns are shelter for fish and small water creatures, and a place for some of them to lay their eggs. Pteridophytes that root in the soft mud of swamps help to stabilize the soil and keep it from being washed away by floods.

Instead of the seasonal changes of spring, summer, autumn, and winter in temperate regions, the tropics have wet and dry seasons. During the wet season, water is plentiful. Rivers flood, and temporary pools and streams fill up again.

water fern (*Ceratopteris thalictroides*)

water clover (*Marsilea* species)

Aquatic ferns

Marsilea and *Ceratopteris* (see above) are found in tropical pools and still lakesides. Water clovers (*Marsilea* species, above left) have creeping stems. Their fronds are upright and free-standing on marshy ground, but their leaflets spread and float on the surface of pools and flood water.

Ceratopteris species have floating fronds and also root into the mud of shallow, still waters. Only the fertile, spore-producing fronds emerge from the surface of the water. *C. thalictroides* (see above right) is so well adapted to living in temporary pools that it can complete its life cycle in three and a half months!

16

Quillworts (*Isoetes* species)

Little is known about quillworts because many of them grow on the bottoms of lakes. The only sign they are there are the "quills" that have broken off and floated to shore. Quillworts such as *Isoetes lacustris* (see below), found in North America and Europe, live in mountain pools or lakes with clear, cold water that is low in nutrients.

Free-floating

Azolla (see below) and *Salvinia* species are free-floating ferns that never take root. They can spread across the surface of tropical lakes very rapidly. This can be a nuisance. For example *Salvinia molesta*, originally from Brazil, is now found on many tropical lakes where it chokes dams and waterways. It has become known as Kariba weed.

Water horsetail (*Equisetum fluviatile*)

This plant is often very abundant in swampy shallow water at the edges of lakes and ponds or in ditches. It is a very hardy horsetail and is found in Iceland, arctic Russia, northern Canada and Alaska, as well as much farther south in the U.S. and Europe. Water horsetail grows in nutrient-rich water in lowland lakes and also in mountain pools or lochs.

It has creeping underground stems, called **rhizomes**, that grow deep in stagnant mud or silt. Air passes down the hollow stems into the rhizomes. Sometimes, like other horsetails, the stiff stems have whorls of branches – but they may also be completely branchless.

WOODLAND FERNS

In the temperate regions of the world, ferns grow best in damp places, especially in mild, moist woods. In the deciduous woods of North America, western Europe, and parts of Asia, the leafy canopy helps to keep the forest floor moist in summer. In autumn, many ferns shed their fronds so that the plants are not damaged by winds or cold weather.

Once the woodlands of the eastern states of the U.S and Britain covered much more of the country than they do today. Vast areas have been cleared to provide land for farming and spreading cities and towns. The pteridophytes once so common in the forests have also been greatly reduced. Wild and domestic grazing animals also threaten fern numbers, so that habitats such as steep-sided valleys and ravines, fence lines, and even gardens become quite important. Where woods have become thin and sparse, bracken fern (see p. 32) has often taken over.

male fern

autumn fern

giant wood fern

Polypodium

Common ferns

Most woodland ferns are hardy plants often with tough, leathery fronds. *Dryopteris* species are common in woods throughout the northern hemisphere. Many are widespread species that can grow in most soils, for example the male fern (*Dryopteris filix-mas*). The giant wood fern (*Dryopteris goldiana*) and the marginal wood fern (*Dryopteris marginalis*) are found only in North American woods, where the crested fern (*Dryopteris cristata*) also grows. In Japan and China, two common species are the autumn fern (*Dryopteris erythrosora*) and *Dryopteris sieboldii*. Very few ferns of temperate woods grow as epiphytes on tree trunks and branches. The polypodies (*Polypodium* species) are an exception, and will grow on walls and banks, as well as on trees.

18

Temperate rain forests

Some coastal regions have such a moist climate that they are often called temperate rain forests. These forests often have a mixture of deciduous and evergreen conifer trees, and are found in Japan, South Island (New Zealand), Tasmania, southern Chile, and the western coastal strip of the U.S. (see right). Ferns like the Pacific coast sword fern (*Polystichum munitum*), together with mosses and lichens, are an important part of the vegetation.

Northern conifer forests

The dark forest floor of the northern conifer forests of North America, Europe, and Asia are not suitable for many forest-floor plants. Ferns such as oak fern (*Gymnocarpium dryopteris*) and beech fern (*Phegopteris connectilis*) are common in damp places (see below).

The great horsetail

The great horsetail (*Equisetum telmateia*, see below) makes a forest of its own in wet, clay hollows in woods. It has shoots that grow up to 8 feet long! It is a European horsetail, although a very similar kind grows in the western coastal strip of North America.

beech fern   oak fern

great horsetail

THE FERN PLANT

Almost all ferns are **perennials**, that is, they live for a number of years. Some are evergreen and have leafy fronds all through the year. Others are deciduous and lose their fronds at certain seasons.

Fern roots sprout from the underground stems of the fern plant, or sometimes from the leaf bases. They are tough and fibrous, and anchor the plant firmly onto a tree or to the ground, absorbing water and mineral nutrients.

Fern stems are called rhizomes. They are usually subterranean (below the soil surface), but epiphytic ferns often have aerial (in the air) rhizomes that creep over the surface of the tree trunk support.

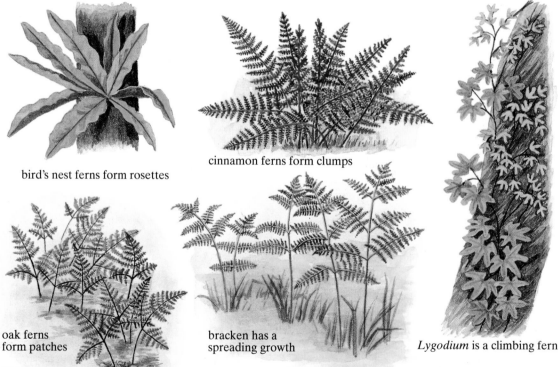

bird's nest ferns form rosettes

cinnamon ferns form clumps

oak ferns form patches

bracken has a spreading growth

Lygodium is a climbing fern

Different forms

Some kinds of ferns have very short, upright stems hidden among the surrounding leaf bases. Ferns with very short stems grow into clumps or tufts, and sometimes neat rosettes.

Ferns with creeping underground rhizomes either send up fronds very close together to make a dense patch, for example, the oak fern (*Gymnocarpium dryopteris*), or at more widely spaced intervals, as seen in bracken (*Pteridium aquilinum*). More unusual growth patterns are shown by the stag's horn ferns, and climbing ferns such as *Lygodium*. The stilt fern (*Oleandra neriiformis*) has spreading rhizomes that are supported above the ground on long stiltlike roots.

The fern frond

This is made up of a leaf **blade** and a leaf stalk or **stipe**. The stipe is often covered in papery scales, but may be smooth or even spiny, as in the prickly stemmed tree fern (*Cnemidaria horrida*). The leaf blade may be simple or divided into leaflets called **pinnae**. The pinnae are often divided into smaller leaflets called **pinnule**s. The **rachis** is the midrib of the leaf.

Unlike the rest of the pteridophytes, the ferns have branching leaf veins. However, all pteridophytes have xylem and phloem tubes in their fronds, rhizomes, and roots. Xylem carry water from the roots to the leaves, the phloem take the sugars made by photosynthesis in the leaf to all other parts of the fern plant.

The leaves are covered with a waxy, waterproof layer called the **cuticle**. This keeps too much water from being lost from the leaf in dry conditions. Tiny holes called **stomata**, through which gases and water vapor pass, are scattered over the lower surface of the leaf.

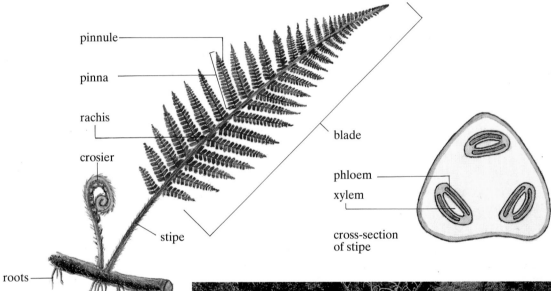

pinnule
pinna
rachis
crosier
stipe
roots
blade
phloem
xylem
cross-section of stipe

Tree ferns

These ferns have upright, woody stems (see right). Growth is from the top, and tree fern trunks cannot grow a little thicker every year as an oak or pine tree does. The outer layer of the trunk shows the scars left by old, fallen fronds. It may be rough and scaly or softly hairy. *Cyathea baileyana* is called the wig tree fern because the top part of its trunk is covered with a shaggy, wiglike growth. New leaves grow from the top of the trunk to make a crown of fronds.

THE FERN FROND

Each kind of fern has its own individual frond shape. A mature plant has fertile fronds, which bear spores that can grow into new plants, and sterile fronds that do not bear spores. In the majority of ferns like *Dryopteris*, these are exactly the same shape, with clusters of spore cases (see p. 28) on the underside of the fertile frond. In some ferns the fertile and sterile fronds look different. Sterile fronds are often arching, with broad leaflets, and fertile fronds are erect, with narrow spore-bearing leaflets.

A few ferns, such as the silver fern (*Pityrogramma calomelanos*) secrete, or ooze out, specks of wax from tiny hairs on their surface. These waxy specks may be white, yellow, or pink.

When the fronds of some ferns are bruised or crushed they scent the air. Anyone walking through waist-high bracken will soon notice its slightly pungent smell, which some people find pleasant. More pleasant smells come from hay-scented ferns such as *Dennstaedtia punctiloba* in the U.S. and *Dryopteris aemula* in Europe.

All shapes
The symmetrical and very attractive shape of fern fronds means that they are very popular with gardeners and houseplant enthusiasts. There is a very wide range in the shape of the leaves, from simple, unlobed blades to those finely divided into many small leaflets.

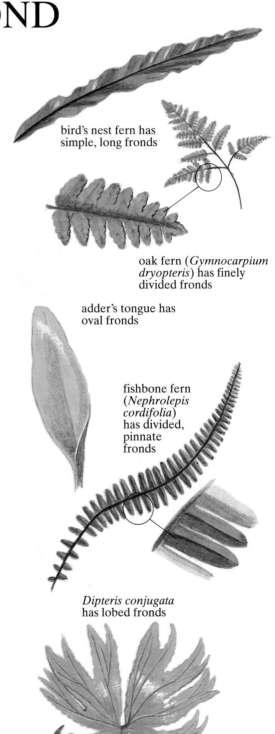

bird's nest fern has simple, long fronds

oak fern (*Gymnocarpium dryopteris*) has finely divided fronds

adder's tongue has oval fronds

fishbone fern (*Nephrolepis cordifolia*) has divided, pinnate fronds

Dipteris conjugata has lobed fronds

Crosiers

New frond buds take a long time to form. They develop on the fern rhizome. When it is time for a new frond to appear, growth can be very rapid as the stipe lengthens and the frond unfurls. Each bud is a tightly coiled frond called a crosier or fiddlehead. A close look shows that each leaflet, although tiny and tightly rolled, is perfectly formed and just waiting to expand.

Water ferns

The floating plants of *Salvinia* are well adapted to their watery home. Groups of three leaves grow along the thin stem. Two leaves of each group contain large air spaces and act as buoys. The third leaf is completely different. It is divided into many threadlike, hairy lobes. These dangle down, absorbing water and nutrients, since *Salvinia* does not have real roots.

scaly crosiers
(*Cyathea*)

hairy crosiers
(soft ground fern,
Hypolepis tenuifolia)

smooth crosiers
(*Microlepia platyphylla*)

Filmy ferns

These extremely fragile ferns (see left) have leaf blades only one cell thick. Water vapor and gases pass in and out over the whole leaf surface, and there are no stomata. This means that water can be lost very rapidly, and filmy ferns quickly shrivel in all but the most humid (moist) conditions. Humidity is the amount of water vapor held in the air. Warm air can hold more than cold air, which is why tropical rain forests support most of the world's filmy ferns, as well as other delicate ferns and mosses.

OTHER PTERIDOPHYTES

The other pteridophytes are club mosses, quillworts, and horsetails. Clubmosses have creeping branched stems that spread over the surface of the ground. Small roots grow along these stems to anchor the plants, and to take up water and nutrients from the soil. There are other branches that grow more or less upright.

The quillwort stem is very short and upright. From its base grow thin branched roots. From the apex, or top, of the stem a dense rosette of leaves is produced.

The horsetails are a distinctive and easily recognizable group of pteridophytes. They are spreading plants that grow into a conspicuous forest of dense stems. The creeping, branched rhizomes are hidden below ground. They are long and tough, and roots sprout at intervals along their length. Some horsetails have food-storage organs, which look like small potatoes, called **tubers**.

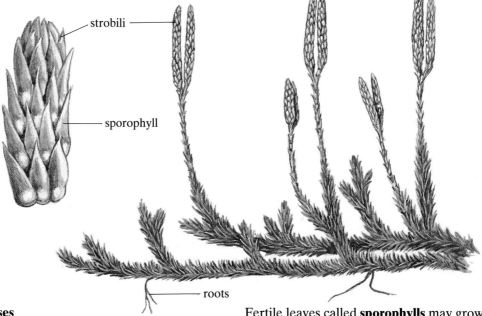

strobili

sporophyll

roots

Club mosses

All stems bear leaves, but the upright shoots are very leafy. These little leaves are roughly spear-shaped, with a single vein or midrib. They are arranged spirally around the stems. The leaves, stems, and roots of club mosses, like the rest of the pteridophytes, contain vascular, or conducting, strands.

Fertile leaves called **sporophylls** may grow in patches along the branches. In stag's horn club moss, as well as in many other kinds, the sporophylls are arranged in conelike **strobili**. These are at the tips of the upright branches, either singly or in twos or threes. In tassel ferns, the strobili hang down at the ends of the drooping stems.

Aerial shoots grow up from the horsetail rhizome. They are stiff, tubular, and jointed. The stems are hollow, with long air canals. Some horsetails, for example, the Dutch rush (*Equisetum hyemale*), do not branch, but most have whorls of branches at each node. The whole plant is stiff and tough because there is a lot of silica (the mineral of which sand is made) in the outer layer of the stems and branches.

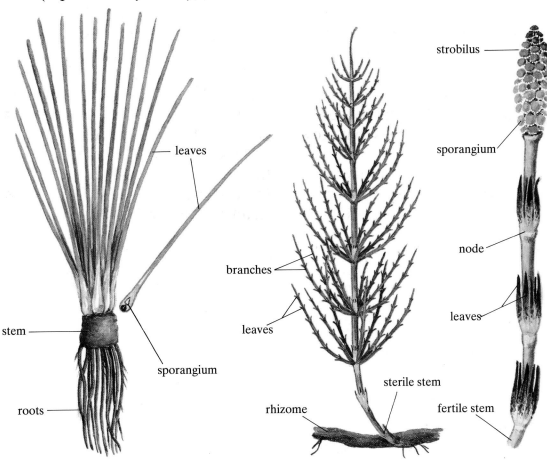

Quillworts

In some quillwort species, the leaves are only a few inches in length and are very narrow. Those of *Isoetes lacustris* are up to 8 inches long. They are quill-shaped, pointed at the tip, and have swollen bases. Inside the leaves are long air spaces.

The swollen leaf bases contain the spore-producing parts of quillwort plants. Most kinds of quillwort are perennial, but older leaves are shed each year. The spores are not released until these leaves break off.

Horsetails

Horsetail leaves are small, papery, pointed scales joined together at their bases to make a whorl at each joint or **node**. Photosynthesis takes place in the green stems and branches, since there is no chlorophyll in the leaves. The erect stems are either sterile or fertile. Fertile stems have strobili at their tips, and are sometimes without branches. They are usually produced at particular times of year. The brown fertile shoots of common horsetail (*Equisetum arvense*) are seen in early spring. Later, the green sterile shoots appear.

LIFE CYCLES

The fern plant is a sporophyte, which produces spores when mature. The spores develop in a **sporangium**, or spore-case, which is an extremely small capsule. Several of these are clustered together, usually on the underside of the leaf blade, in a special fertile spot called a **sorus**. When ripe, the spores are released.

Spores that land in a damp spot soon germinate (start to grow), but they do not grow into a new fern plant. The spore grows into a thin, green heart-shaped plant only about a quarter inch across – the prothallus. It is all that remains of the gametophyte stage of the life cycle, which produces the male and female sex cells. At the pointed end, male sex cells form, and in the notch of the "heart," female sex cells form in special, extremely small pockets.

When the ripe male cells are released, they swim toward a ripe female cell. A film of water around the prothallus is vital; without it the male cells cannot swim, and the whole plantlet dries up and dies. As soon as the first female cell is fertilized by joining with a male cell, it begins to grow. The prothallus dies and the new little plant gradually develops into an actual fern plant.

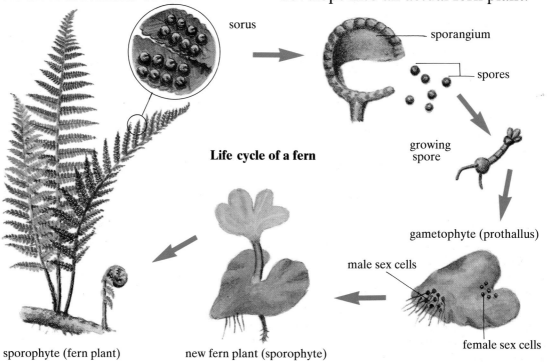

sorus

sporangium

spores

Life cycle of a fern

growing spore

gametophyte (prothallus)

male sex cells

female sex cells

sporophyte (fern plant)

new fern plant (sporophyte)

Spikemoss and quillworts

Quillwort spore cases are hidden in the swollen base of each leaf. Unlike the rest of the pteridophytes, spikemosses and quillworts produce different-sized spores – very tiny microspores and larger megaspores. When these germinate, the microspores produce male and the megaspores produce female prothalli. The male sex cells have to swim to a different prothallus to fertilize the female egg.

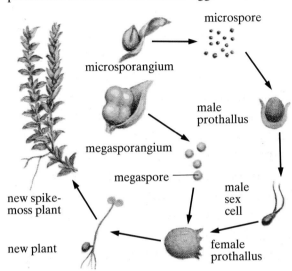

- microspore
- microsporangium
- male prothallus
- megasporangium
- megaspore
- male sex cell
- new spike-moss plant
- new plant
- female prothallus

Spores galore!

The spore cases of ferns like *Dryopteris* (see below) develop on the underside of the frond in a distinct cluster, called a sorus.

Club mosses, quillworts, and horsetails

The life cycles of these other pteridophytes follow the same pattern as that of the ferns, but there are a few differences. The spore-cases are not arranged in clusters, or sori. Instead, they are protected by a leaflike sporophyll, which may not contain chlorophyll. In most club mosses (*Lycopodium* species) and all spikemosses (*Selaginella* species) and horsetails (*Equisetum* species), the sporophylls are all grouped together in strobili.

A *Lycopodium* club moss spore takes as long as seven years to germinate! During this time, it lies dormant, and is gradually buried by a build-up of dead leaves and soil. When it starts to grow, it becomes associated with an underground fungus. Far from doing it harm, the fungus helps the club moss prothallus to absorb nutrients. The prothallus (see right) grows into a lobed, white tuberlike plant about an inch across. It is also slow to develop, and may not produce sex cells for another 15 years.

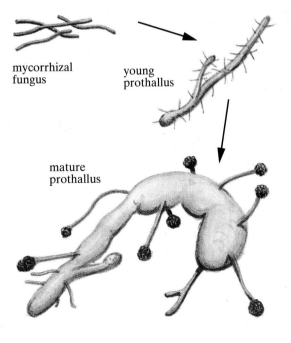

- mycorrhizal fungus
- young prothallus
- mature prothallus

SPREADING SPORES

A fern plant produces truly huge numbers of spore cases every year, and in each one there are hundreds of minute, single-celled spores. A few ferns release their spores through slits in their large spore cases. Most others have smaller spore cases, and they have a different way of opening to release their spores. Those with sporangia in groups sometimes have a thin protective flap, the **indusium**, that covers each sorus.

Each spore case is joined to the frond by a tiny stalk. The spore-containing sac has a special ring of dead cells around the outside, called the **annulus**. These cells have very thin outer walls and thick inner ones and are filled with water. In dry conditions, water evaporates through the thin walls of the annulus. As it does so, the side walls of these cells are pulled closer together, putting pressure on the annulus. This pressure bursts the spore case at a very weak spot – the **stomium**. This happens suddenly, and the light spores are catapulted out of the sporangium and into the air. When the annulus cells are completely dry, it flicks back again, shooting out any remaining spores.

Fern spores are usually brown, black, or yellow in color. On a very still day, many settle quite close to the parent plant. On a breezy day they are carried far and wide. It is a very effective way of spreading spores, but most of them land in the wrong place and fail to grow.

Release mechanisms

Some groups have quite large, round spore cases that open by slits or pores. In *Ophioglossum* these grow in rows on a spike (see below).

A fern sporangium

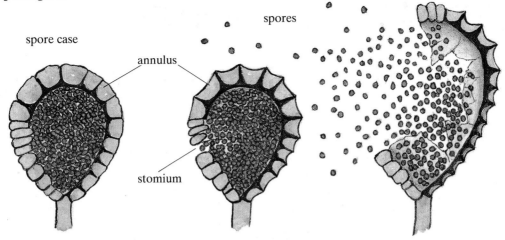

spore case

spores

annulus

stomium

Vegetative Reproduction
Some ferns multiply not by spores but by dividing off new plantlets. This is called **vegetative reproduction**. Because no sex cells are involved, it is also known as asexual reproduction. Ferns that multiply vegetatively are found as colonies – lots of plants of the same kind growing close together.

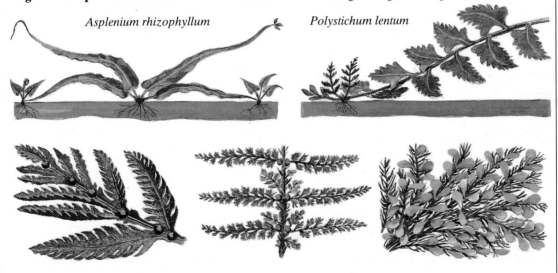

Asplenium rhizophyllum

Polystichum lentum

Tectaria gemmifera

Polystichum setiferum

Asplenium daucifolium

Ferns such as *Asplenium rhizophyllum* produce tiny new plantlets at the tips of the fronds where they touch the ground. The little plants take root and begin to grow independently. Small buds or bulbils develop on the fronds of some ferns. Sometimes these bulbils drop off before beginning to develop further (*Tectaria gemmifera*).

Others start to sprout fronds while attached to the parent frond. The weight of the plantlets bends the frond to the ground. It rots away, and the new ferns grow. These plantlets form near the frond tips of *Polystichum lentum*, along the rachis of the soft shield fern (*Polystichum setiferum*), and all over the surface of *Asplenium daucifolium*.

HOW FERNS SURVIVE

The ideal conditions for ferns to grow well are a warm, damp climate and enough light for photosynthesis. Places where these conditions are found, the tropics and subtropics, have the highest numbers of fern species. About 75 percent of the world's ferns are found in the tropics. Jamaica, a tropical island in the West Indies can boast about 500 fern species, whereas the entire continental U.S. has only 207. Ferns and their relatives are still plentiful in less favorable climates, though. How do they survive adverse conditions?

Life in the cold

Winters get colder the farther from the equator you travel, and high mountainsides are also cold. Plants that grow in these regions have to survive frost, snow, and freezing winds. Ferns die back at the end of summer. The dead fronds do not drop off but collapse over the base of the plant (see above). This insulates the living underground parts of the fern from frost damage.

Surviving in the dark

Warmth and moisture are characteristic of the tropical rain forests, but on the forest floor and in valleys and rocky ravines there is very little light indeed. Ferns such as the maidenhair (see above) contain other pigments to trap all the light energy that reaches the dim forest floor. These pigments are red, so the fronds of these ferns are tinged reddish or pink.

No water!

Australia, Africa, Mexico, and the southwestern U.S. all have very warm regions with a long, dry season. The ferns that grow in these dry or semiarid climates manage to overcome drought by conserving as much water as possible. They root in the shadow of boulders or beside rocks. Their fronds are small and are often covered with white hairs or scales, which reflect heat and also trap water vapor as in the resurrection fern (*Polypodium polypodiodes*, see right). In extremely dry seasons, some ferns lose their fronds and survive as underground rhizomes until the rains fall again.

A few remarkable ferns of dry places, like the resurrection fern (*Paraceterach muelleri*) from Australia, spend the dry season as a mass of brittle, brown fronds – to all appearances quite dead. A short while after the rains come, however, these fronds turn green again and the leaflets expand.

Stagnant water

Plants as well as animals need to **respire**, or breathe. Oxygen gas, present in the air, is essential for this to occur. Even roots have to breathe, which is why most plants cannot live in the stagnant mud of swamps and bogs that contains little oxygen. The plants that can survive there have ways of overcoming this problem.

One way is to have hollow stems. Horsetails all have hollow canals down to their rhizomes, deep underground. Plants, such as water horsetail (shown below), also have hollow rhizomes so that oxygen can pass right down to the roots. When the stems die in autumn, they break off just above water level to leave a breathing tube.

summer

winter

BRACKEN

One of the five most common plants in the world is bracken (*Pteridium aquilinum*). It is found in all parts of the world where conditions are suitable. Most botanists agree that, although widespread, all bracken belongs to one species. It varies a bit from place to place, however, so the bracken found in New Zealand is not quite the same as that of Europe.

When human populations were small, and thick forests covered huge tracts of land in both tropical and temperate regions, bracken was only found on the edges of woodlands.

Ever since the Stone Age, people have cleared more and more forests for crops and domestic animals. Bracken grows well in these light, open conditions and so spreads rapidly. Today, it is often the main plant of dry grasslands, heaths, moors, and lower mountain slopes.

From a single spore, a bracken plant can grow and spread as its tough, branched rhizomes creep through the soil. Eventually a patch of bracken from one spore can cover a large area – research in Finland showed that one patch covered over 53,000 square miles.

Bracken and fire

If a fire breaks out on a heath or moorland, bracken is often already growing there. As the bracken rhizomes may be 20 inches or more below ground, they escape unharmed, and new fronds spring up with renewed vigor after the fire (see right).

After a forest fire, the land is open and bare, with a surface layer of ash rich in minerals. These are ideal conditions for bracken spores to germinate and grow, thus starting up new bracken colonies.

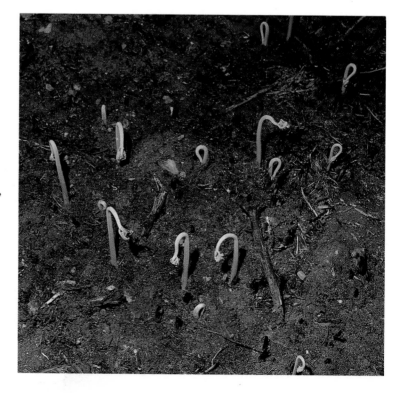

Deadly food

Bracken is poisonous and tastes bad; usually domestic animals will not eat it. Therefore, they overgraze the bracken-free parts of their pasture (see right). This is a great problem on hill pastures, but the control of bracken is difficult and expensive. Unfortunately, animals sometimes eventually develop a taste for bracken. If there is nothing else to eat, they are driven by hunger to feed on it. Horses die quickly from bracken poisoning, but cattle and sheep do not become ill right away. They develop cancers of the mouth, gullet, and stomach from which they die.

In Venezuela and Costa Rica, people who drank milk from bracken-fed cattle have also developed these cancers. In Japan, young fronds are eaten as a vegetable, and many people develop stomach cancer that may be due to this diet. In Britain, people have been advised not to walk through bracken in late summer when the spores are released into the air. Forestry workers wear face masks at this time so that they do not breathe in the spores.

A dense canopy
In midsummer the dense thicket of bracken fronds screens most of the light from the ground below (see left). In winter they die down, but the dead fronds build up a thick layer over the ground. Smaller plants cannot compete, and most die out.

THREATENED HABITATS

The plant communities of remote places such as islands are interesting and unique. They frequently contain a high proportion of fern species, because fern spores are so light that they are carried from distant lands by the wind.

If you look at an atlas, you will see that there are subtropical and tropical islands in the Pacific, Atlantic, and Indian Oceans. They are often small and are mostly volcanic in origin. Sometimes the volcanoes are still active, but other islands are the remains of volcanoes that have been extinct (dead) for centuries. Many of these islands are a long way from the nearest continent.

Some island plants, including ferns, have been isolated from the place where they originally came from for such a long time that they have gradually changed, or **evolved**, into quite separate species. Many of these are found nowhere else in the world, and are known as **endemics**.

St. Helena

This is a small island in the tropical Atlantic Ocean. Although rugged and hilly, it had a unique and rich vegetation until goats were introduced in 1513. These multiplied so rapidly that they virtually destroyed the plant life before any botanists had been able to visit the island. Today (see above), the remnants of the native ferns and flowering plants are found only on the highest and most inaccessible peaks and ravines.

Flying animals such as birds, insects, and bats can find their way to distant islands, but most mammals cannot cross the sea and so are not a natural part of the islands' animal life. However, rabbits, pigs, donkeys, and goats all arrived in the ships of early explorers and traders, either when they landed deliberately or when they were shipwrecked! They all graze on plants, but goats are the biggest menace. They are hardy, agile, and breed quickly. They can climb almost anywhere and are not fussy eaters. They tend to destroy much of the natural vegetation.

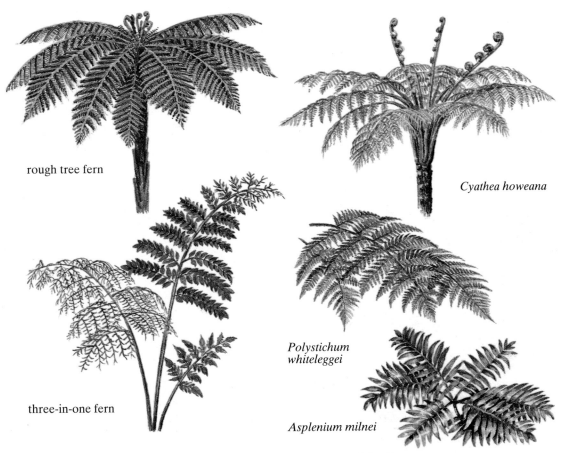

rough tree fern

three-in-one fern

Cyathea howeana

Polystichum whiteleggei

Asplenium milnei

Norfolk Island

This tiny island in the southwest Pacific Ocean has lost almost all of its vegetation because people have cleared it for farming. Fortunately, part of it has been made into a national park, where many plants, including ferns (see above) such as rough tree fern (*Cyathea australis*) and the three-in-one fern (*Asplenium dimorphum*), are now protected.

Lord Howe Island

This is a tiny island in the southwest Pacific Ocean that has escaped the influence of people and their domestic animals. It has 48 native ferns, including 17 endemic species; a few are shown here (see above). It is hoped it will remain unspoiled, as the Lord Howe group of islands is a World Heritage Site, and over half the island itself is a permanent park reserve.

NEW "HOMES"

When temperate woodlands are cleared for farming and building, many other plants and animals that are a part of this kind of habitat are destroyed. Ferns are threatened in two ways. They lose a place to grow and are eaten by browsing domestic animals. They are very slow to recover from overgrazing. Many woodland species now grow only in deep ravines or plots of land unsuitable for plowing.

Shoulders and fence lines dividing fields and bordering roads are good sites for woodland ferns. Steep road shoulders are very characteristic of rural Europe. They are so familiar that it is easy to forget that they were built by people many years ago. Ferns such as the polypodies flourish on road shoulders, as do hart's tongue fern (*Phyllitis scolopendrium*) and soft shield fern (*Polystichum setiferum*).

common horsetail

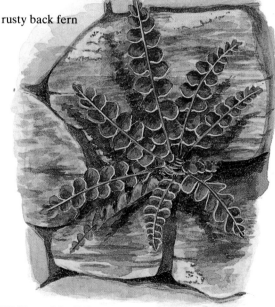

rusty back fern

Gardens
The disturbed loamy soil of gardens, plant nurseries, and arable fields is an ideal environment for the common horsetail (*Equisetum arvense*, see above). This is one of the few pteridophyte "pests" – it grows as a weed worldwide! It is very difficult to get rid of because its tough rhizomes grow deep in the soil, and it is resistant to many chemical herbicides.

Walls and buildings
Old stone walls and buildings are good sites for ferns. Although most of the species found are plants of naturally dry, rocky places, some have become far more common on walls than in their natural environment. The rusty back fern (*Ceterach officinarum*, see above) is found far beyond its geographical range on walls in Britain and Europe.

marsh horsetail

fir club moss

forked club moss

Industrial sites

Slag heaps, quarries, mineshafts, and abandoned sites do not seem likely places for plants to live, but some ferns, club mosses, and horsetails are among the first plants to grow on and colonize these industrial wastelands.

One of the few plants able to colonize coal slag heaps is the common horsetail. Its tangled rhizomes bind loose rocks, sending up lots of new shoots every year. In wet hollows, marsh horsetail (*Equisetum palustre*) grows. On the flat tops of old slag heaps, colonies of moonwort are sometimes seen. As the air pollution over industrialized areas has decreased in recent years, more sensitive plants such as forked club moss (*Lycopodium clavatum*) and fir club moss (*Huperzia selago*) are becoming common (see above).

Old quarries

Limestone has been mined for a very long time. Lime has always had many uses, including cement making and in whitewash paints. The lime was made by baking limestone in kilns near the quarries.

Around the lime kilns, the fine limy slag clogs the soil. Here, and in puddles and shallow floodwater at the bottom of the old quarries, adder's tongue and moonwort (see left) ferns grow among grasses. As these species are becoming rare in their natural habitat of damp, unplowed grassland, these no longer used sites are valuable as new habitats.

PLANTS THAT MADE COAL

Most of the world's coal deposits are the remains of plants that grew in the Carboniferous Era. This began about 345 million years ago, and lasted 65 million years. The climate was warm and humid and much of the land was low-lying and often flooded. It was not separated into continents as it is now but was one huge land mass called Pangaea. Across this land, there were vast swamps. The plants of the Carboniferous swamps were very different indeed from the plants of any swamps found today.

The world in the Carboniferous Era

China
North America
Europe
South America
Africa
India
Antarctica
Australia

Today

Carboniferous Swamps

The main plants growing in these swamps were tall club moss trees such as *Sigillaria* and *Lepidodendron*. Club mosses are all small leafy plants today, but *Lepidodendron* was about 175 feet high, far taller than most living broad-leaved trees! *Sigillaria* was slightly shorter. Other trees that were found in these swamps were *Calamites*, an ancestor of the horsetail up to 30 feet tall, and *Psaronius*, a 25 foot-tall tree fern. These tree ferns are more closely related to the living tropical fern *Marattia* than to living tree ferns, however.

On the swampy forest floor, smaller plants scrambled over the fallen trees and living tree trunks. These included *Sphenophyllum*, a horsetail, and *Selaginites* – plants very similar to spikemosses (*Selaginella* species). These smaller plants probably made a green blanket over the ground and in the water.

Coal formation

For 65 million years, these ancient plants lived and died, and eventually sank into the marshy ground. Plants do not decay properly in bogs and swamps because there is not enough oxygen in the stagnant water to allow the microorganisms that cause decay to live and multiply. The half-rotten vegetation gradually builds up into a thick layer (see 1 below).

This process can be seen in peat bogs today. In fact, peat is the first stage of coal formation, but today's peat consists of the remains of mosses (*Sphagnum* species) and flowering plants such as sedges and grasses. Modern pteridophytes have only a small part in peat formation now.

The Carboniferous peats were covered with mud and silt. Heat and pressure changed the peat into coal (see 2 below).

1 swamp	
decaying vegetation	river
rock	
2 mud and silt compress the peat to form coal	
peat	
rock	

THE GREENHOUSE EFFECT

The Chinese were probably the first people to use coal for fuel, about 3,000 years ago. The demand for coal rose sharply in the 1700s, during the beginning of the Industrial Revolution. In 1900, world coal production was 833 million tons. In 1980, this had risen to 3.8 billion tons! Even so, there is enough coal to last for perhaps another 400 years, and possibly more deposits are yet to be discovered.

The U.S., China, and the Soviet Union produce the most coal, but many other countries also mine coal. Most coal is used to fuel power stations that generate electricity. It is also used as a domestic fuel. Coke, which is specially heated coal, is used in the manufacture of steel. Many industries use chemicals made from coal tar.

Uses of coal tar
Coal tar, which is made from coal, has many uses, some of which are shown below. None of these products could be made without the plants that lived so long ago – the remains of which formed the coal we use today (see p. 38).

tar and creosote

explosives and chemicals

antiseptics and medicines

nail varnish and perfumes

pesticides, herbicides, and fertilizers

nylon, synthetic rubber, and plastics

saccharin

The Greenhouse Effect

During the long Carboniferous period, enormous amounts of carbon dioxide gas were removed from the atmosphere and "locked up" as carbon compounds in the swamp vegetation. When coal and other **fossil fuels** like oil and natural gas are burned, the carbon dioxide that was taken out of the atmosphere by the living plants millions of years ago is suddenly put back into the air. As the demand for energy rises, the rate at which the locked-up carbon dioxide is released is also increased. At the same time, the forests that would help to use up some of the extra carbon dioxide are being cut down. Although opinions are divided, an increasing number of scientists believe that this sudden input of carbon dioxide is affecting the world's climate.

More carbon dioxide means that more of the sun's energy is retained, and so the atmosphere gets warmer. This is known as the greenhouse effect.

Carbon dioxide and a few other gases that are being released into the air (nitrous oxide, ozone, methane, and chlorofluorocarbons) are known as the "greenhouse gases." No one knows exactly what will happen to the world's climate if the scientists are right, but many things may occur (see the illustrations below).

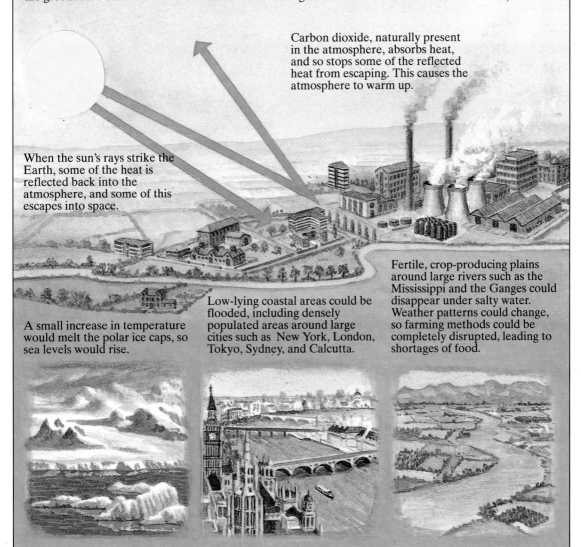

Carbon dioxide, naturally present in the atmosphere, absorbs heat, and so stops some of the reflected heat from escaping. This causes the atmosphere to warm up.

When the sun's rays strike the Earth, some of the heat is reflected back into the atmosphere, and some of this escapes into space.

A small increase in temperature would melt the polar ice caps, so sea levels would rise.

Low-lying coastal areas could be flooded, including densely populated areas around large cities such as New York, London, Tokyo, Sydney, and Calcutta.

Fertile, crop-producing plains around large rivers such as the Mississippi and the Ganges could disappear under salty water. Weather patterns could change, so farming methods could be completely disrupted, leading to shortages of food.

USES OF FERNS

Ferns are attractive plants to have in gardens, beside pools, in rock gardens, and in houses and greenhouses. Fern mania swept Britain in the late 1800s. Wealthy households kept delicate and exotic ferns in ornate glass cabinets called "wardian" cases. These kept the ferns moist and safely screened from smoky coal fires. The collectors took ferns from the countryside to put into their gardens.

The trade in ferns continues to flourish because people in countries all around the world have the time and money to buy unusual plants for their enjoyment. Today, however, there is no excuse for taking wild plants. Ferns can be propagated, or multiplied, by specialist gardeners from spores, bulbils, or by dividing up larger plants. New methods of tissue culture are used to grow some kinds of ferns. Tissue culture is carried out in special containers in a laboratory. Hundreds of new plantlets can be grown from tiny slithers of a parent fern.

Fern food

The young crosiers of a number of ferns are eaten in many different countries but are most popular in southeastern Asia and Pacific islands. The Maoris of New Zealand are fond of them, too. They are cooked or eaten raw, and a few kinds are packaged and sold commercially. In the U.S., the young fronds of ostrich fern (*Matteuccia struthiopteris*, see right) are sold as a delicacy. The ferns most often eaten in Asia and the Pacific islands are the climbing swamp vine fern (*Stenochlaena palustris*), *Helminthostachys zeylanica*, the vegetable fern (*Diplazium esculentum*), and the water fern (*Ceratopteris thalictroides*).

Some ferns are used as natural medicines. They are supposed to be very effective in getting rid of intestinal worms. In developed countries, the use of ferns to treat worms has been discontinued in favor of modern drugs, but in parts of the world where herbalism and folk medicine are still important, ferns are still used in this way.

Uses of Ferns

Rural people have always been good at using what nature provided. In the past pteridophytes have been put to a number of local uses.

bracken was used as bedding

packing

bracken was burned, producing potash which was used for:

tanning leather

added to fats to make soap

added to sand to make glass

The green fronds of bracken were once used in Europe to package fruit and fish, both to prevent bruising and to keep insects away. The dry fronds were once widely used as bedding for animals and as a mattress stuffing for people! The poisons in bracken fronds probably helped to kill fleas. Dry fronds were also burned, and the potash-rich ash was collected and used in various ways (see above).

Horsetails contain so much silica that their shoots were once used in the way that very fine sandpaper is used today. It gave the finishing touch to wood and metal implements, including musical instruments. The Dutch rush (*Equisetum hyemale*) was particularly useful.

Horsetails and ferns were also used to dye wool in the 1300s (see above). The club mosses alpine club moss (*Diphasiastrum alpinum*), stag's horn club moss (*Lycopodium clavatum*), and fir club moss (*Huperzia selago*), though possibly used as dye plants, were mostly used as mordants to make the color "fast" so that it would not wash out. The final color depends on the mordant used.

GLOSSARY

ANNULUS – The row of cells around a fern spore case that catapults out the spores when it dries out.

BLADE – The flat part of a leaf.

CHLOROPHYLL – The green pigment in plants that uses the energy in sunlight to make food by photosynthesis.

CUTICLE – A waxy, waterproof layer that covers the surface of most plants.

ENDEMIC – A species of plant or animal found naturally in only one particular country or island.

EPIPHYTE – A plant that grows in the air supported by other plants.

EVOLVE – To change gradually and naturally, usually over a long period of time.

FOSSIL FUELS – Fuels such as coal, oil, and natural gas that are the remains of plants that lived millions of years ago.

GAMETOPHYTE – The stage in a plant's life cycle that bears the male and female sex organs.

GERMINATION – The sprouting of a seed to give a new plant.

HABITAT – The natural home of a plant or animal.

INDUSIUM – A small thin flap that covers the clusters of spore cases (sori) of some ferns.

NODE – The part of a stem where leaves or branches sprout.

PERENNIAL – A plant that lives for many years.

PHLOEM – Special tubes that conduct sugars from the leaves to all other parts of the plant.

PHOTOSYNTHESIS – The process in chlorophyll-containing plants that uses sunlight to convert carbon dioxide gas and water into sugars, releasing oxygen.

PINNA (plural pinnae) – Each leaflet seen when a fern frond is divided into two rows of leaflets.

PINNULES – The tiny leaflets seen when each pinna is further divided.

PROTHALLUS – The tiny plantlet that is all that remains of the gametophyte stage of pteridophytes.

PTERIDOPHYTES – The group of plants containing ferns, horsetails, club mosses, and quillworts.

RACHIS – The midrib of the fern leaf.

RESPIRE – To take up oxygen from the environment and use it to power vital life processes of living things.

RHIZOMES – Underground stems, although fern stems that are above ground are also called rhizomes.

SORUS (plural sori) – A cluster of spore cases found on a fern frond.

SPORANGIUM – A spore case.

SPORES – Minute, powdery units produced by nonflowering plants that can grow into new plants.

SPOROPHYLL – A specially modified leaf that bears sporangia, or spore cases.

SPOROPHYTE – The green fern plant that produces spores.

STIPE – The stem of a fern frond.

STOMATA (singular stoma) – Tiny holes in the surface of leaves through which gases and water vapor can pass in and out.

STOMIUM – A weak spot in the wall of a fern spore case that tears when the annulus dries out, releasing the spores.

STROBILI (singular strobilus) – Conelike arrangements of sporophylls.

TUBERS – Swollen underground stems that contain starchy food reserves.

VEGETATIVE REPRODUCTION – The means by which some plants increase their numbers without the formation of sex cells.

XYLEM – Special tubes that conduct water from the roots to all other parts of the plant.

FURTHER READING

For children
Plants by editors of Raintree Pub; Raintree, 1987.
For adults
A Field Guide to Ferns and Their Related Families: Northeastern & Central North America by Boughton Cobb; Houghton Mifflin, 1975.
Encyclopedia of Ferns by David Jones; Timber, 1987.
A Field Manual of the Ferns & Fern Allies of the United States & Canada by David B. Lellinger; Smithsonian, 1985.

FERNS IN THIS BOOK

Acrostichum aureum
Adder's tongue fern (*Ophioglossum vulgatum*)
Alpine club moss (*Diphasiastrum alpinum*)
Alpine water fern (*Blechnum penna-marina*)
Asplenium species (*A. daucifolium, A. milnei, A. rhizophyllum*)
Athyrium distentifolium
Autumn fern (*Dryopteris erythrosora*)
Azolla species
Beech fern (*Phegopteris connectilis*)
Bird's nest fern (*Asplenium nidus*)
Black tree fern (*Cyathea medullaris*)
Bracken (*Pteridium aquilinum*)
Brittle bladder fern (*Cystopteris fragilis*)
Ceratopteris species
Cinnamon fern (*Osmunda cinnamomea*)
Climbing fern (*Lygodium* species)
Club moss (*Lycopodium* species)
Common horsetail (*Equisetum arvense*)
Common maidenhair (*Adiantum capillus-veneris*)
Common polypody (*Polypodium vulgare*)
Common tassel fern (*Lycopodium phlegmaria*)
Crested fern (*Dryopteris cristata*)
Cyathea species (*C. howeana*)
Dipteris conjugata
Dryopteris species (*D. sieboldii*)
Dutch rush (*Equisetum hyemale*)
Elephant's ear fern (*Platycerium elephantotis*)
Elkhorn fern (*Platycerium bifurcatum*)
Filmy ferns (*Hymenophyllum* species)
Fir club moss (*Huperzia selago*)
Fishbone fern (*Nephrolepis cordifolia*)
Forked or stag's horn club moss (*Lycopodium clavatum*)
Fork ferns (*Psilotum* species)
Giant fern (*Angiopteris evecta*)
Giant wood fern (*Dryopteris goldiana*)
Great horsetail (*Equisetum telmateia*)
Green spleenwort (*Asplenium viride*)
Hart's tongue fern (*Phyllitis scolopendrium*)
Hay-scented buckler fern (*Dryopteris aemula*)
Hay-scented fern (*Dennstaedtia punctiloba*)
Helminthostachys zeylanica
Holly fern (*Polystichum lonchitis*)

Kariba weed (*Salvinia molesta*)
Lady ferns (*Athyrium* species)
Maidenhair ferns (*Adiantum* species)
Male fern (*Dryopteris filix-mas*)
Marattia species
Marginal wood fern (*Dryopteris marginalis*)
Marsh horsetail (*Equisetum palustre*)
Marsilea species
Microlepia platyphylla
Moonwort (*Botrychium lunaria*)
Oak fern (*Gymnocarpium dryopteris*)
Ophioglossum species
Ostrich fern (*Matteuccia struthiopteris*)
Pacific coast sword fern (*Polystichum munitum*)
Parsley fern (*Cryptogramma crispa*)
Polypody ferns (*Polypodium* species)
Polystichum species (*P. lentum, P. whiteleggei*)
Prickly shield fern (*Polystichum vestitum*)
Prickly stemmed tree fern (*Cnemidaria horrida*)
Quillworts (*Isoetes* species, *I. lacustris*)
Resurrection fern (*Paraceterach muelleri*)
Resurrection fern (*Polypodium polypodiodes*)
Rough tree fern (*Cyathea australis*)
Royal fern (*Osmunda regalis*)
Rusty back fern (*Ceterach officinarum*)
Salvinia species
Shoestring fern (*Vittaria* species)
Silver fern (*Pityrogramma calomelanos*)
Soft ground fern (*Hypolepis tenuifolia*)
Soft shield fern (*Polystichum setiferum*)
Spikemosses (*Selaginella* species)
Stag's horn fern (*Platycerium* species, *P. andinum*)
Stilt fern (*Oleandra neriiformis*)
Tectaria gemmifera
Three-in-one-fern (*Asplenium dimorphum*)
Umbrella fern (*Gleichenia microphyllum*)
Vegetable fern (*Diplazium esculentum*)
Vine fern (*Stenochlaena palustris*)
Water clover (*Marsilea quadrifolia*)
Water fern (*Ceratopteris thalictroides*)
Water horsetail (*Equisetum fluviatile*)
Wig tree fern (*Cyathea baileyana*)
Wilson's filmy fern (*Hymenophyllum wilsonii*)

INDEX

A

Acrostichum aureum 8
adder's tongue ferns 11, 22, 37
Adiantum capillus-veneris 11
alpine club moss 43
alpine water fern 15
Angiopteris evecta 13
annulus 28, 29
asexual reproduction 29
Asplenium daucifolium 29
Asplenium dimorphum 35
Asplenium milnei 35
Asplenium nidus 13
Asplenium rhizophyllum 29
Asplenium viride 14, 15
Athyrium distentifolium 15
Athyrium species 9
Australian tree fern 10
autumn fern 18
Azolla species 17

B

beech fern 19
bird's nest ferns 13, 20, 22
black tree fern 10
blade 21
Blechnum penna-marina 15
botanists 8, 10, 32, 34
Botrychium lunaria 15
bracken 18, 20, 22, 32-33, 43
brittle bladder fern 14

C

Calamites species 38
canopy 12, 18
carbon dioxide 8, 41
Carboniferous Era 38-39, 41
Ceratopteris thalictroides 16, 42
Ceterach officinarum 36
chlorophyll 8, 25, 27
cinnamon ferns 20
climbing ferns 13, 20, 42
club mosses 6, 8, 9, 13, 24, 27,
    38, 43

Cnemidaria horrida 21
coal 38-39, 40-41
common horsetail 25, 36, 37
common maidenhair 11
common polypody 11
common tassel fern 13
conifer forests 19
crested fern 18
crosiers 21, 23, 42
Cryptogramma crispa 14, 15
cuticle 21
Cyathea australis 35
Cyathea baileyana 21
Cyathea howeana 35
Cyathea medullaris 10
Cyathea species 23
Cystopteris fragilis 14

D

deciduous forests 18-19
Dennstaedtia punctiloba 22
Diphasiastrum alpinum 15, 43
Diplazium esculentum 42
Dipteris conjugata 22
Dryopteris aemula 22
Dryopteris cristata 18
Dryopteris erythrosora 18
Dryopteris filix-mas 18
Dryopteris goldiana 18
Dryopteris marginalis 18
Dryopteris sieboldii 18
Dryopteris species 18, 22, 27
Dutch rush 25, 43
dyes 43

E

elephant's ear fern 12
elkhorn fern 12
endemics 34
epiphytes 12, 13, 18, 20
Equisetum arvense 25, 36
Equisetum fluviatile 17
Equisetum hyemale 25, 43
Equisetum palustre 37

Equisetum species 27
Equisetum telmateia 19
evolution 34

F

fertilization 26-27
filmy ferns 11, 23
fir club moss 37, 43
fishbone fern 22
forked clubmoss 37
fork ferns 6, 8
fossil fuels 38-39, 40-41
free-floating ferns 17
fronds 10-11, 12-13, 15, 16, 21,
    22-23

G

gametophyte 8, 9, 26
germination 14, 26-27, 32
giant fern 13
giant wood fern 18
Gleichenia microphyllum 13
great horsetail 19
greenhouse effect 40-41
green spleenwort 14
Gymnocarpium dryopteris 19,
    20, 22

H

habitats 9, 18, 34-35, 36, 37
hart's tongue fern 36
hay-scented ferns 22
Helminthostachys zeylanica 42
holly fern 15
horsetails 6, 8, 9, 17, 24-25, 27,
    31, 38, 43
Huperzia selago 37, 43
Hymenophyllum wilsonii 11
Hypolepis tenuifolia 23

I

indusium 28
Isoetes lacustris 17, 25
Isoetes species 17

K

Kariba weed 17

L

lady ferns 9
Lepidodendron species 38
Lycopodium clavatum 37, 43
Lycopodium phlegmaria 13
Lycopodium species 9, 27
Lygodium species 13, 20

M

maidenhair ferns 11, 30
Malaysian climbing fern 13
male fern 18
mangrove swamps 8
Marattia species 38
marginal wood fern 18
marsh horsetail 37
Marsilea quadrifolia 11
Marsilea species 11, 16
Matteuccia struthiopteris 42
medicines 42
Microlepia platyphylla 23
moonwort ferns 15, 37
mycorrhizal fungus 27

N

Nephrolepis cordifolia 22
node 25

O

oak ferns 19, 20, 22
Oleandra neriiformis 20
Ophioglossum species 28
Ophioglossum vulgatum 11
Osmunda regalis 11
ostrich fern 42

P

Pacific coast sword fern 19
Paraceterach muelleri 31
parsley fern 14, 15
peat 39
perennials 20
Phegopteris connectilis 19
phloem 8, 9, 21
photosynthesis 8, 9, 21, 25, 30
Phyllitis scolopendrium 36

pinnae 21
pinnules 21
Pityrogramma calomelanos 22
Platycerium andinum 12
Platycerium bifurcatum 12
Platycerium elephantotis 12
Platycerium species 12
poisons 33, 43
pollution 37
polypodies 11, 18, 36
Polypodium polypodioides 31
Polypodium species 11, 18, 36
Polypodium vulgare 11
Polystichum lentum 29
Polystichum lonchitis 15
Polystichum munitum 19
Polystichum setiferum 29, 36
Polystichum vestitum 15
Polystichum whiteleggei 35
prickly shield fern 15
prickly stemmed tree fern 21
propagation 42
prothallus 8, 9, 14, 26, 27
Psaronius species 38
Psilotum species 8
Pteridium aquilinum 20, 32
pteridophytes 8-9, 15, 16-17, 18, 21, 24-25, 27, 36, 39

Q

quillworts 8, 17, 24-25, 27

R

rachis 21, 29
respiration 31
resurrection fern 31
rhizomes 17, 20, 21, 23, 24, 25, 31, 32
rough tree fern 35
royal ferns 11
rusty back fern 36

S

Salvinia molesta 17
Salvinia species 17, 23
Selaginella species 9, 27, 38
Selaginites 38
shoestring ferns 9
Sigillaria species 38

silver fern 22
soft ground fern 23
soft shield fern 29, 36
sorus 26, 27, 28
South American stag's horn 12
Sphenophyllum species 38
spikemosses 9, 27, 38
sporangia 24, 26, 28
spores 8, 10, 11, 13, 14, 16, 22, 25, 26-27, 28-29, 32
sporophylls 24, 27
sporophyte 8, 9, 26
stag's horn ferns 12, 20, 24, 43
Stenochlaena palustris 42
stilt fern 20
stipe 21, 23
stomata 21, 23
stomium 28
strobili 6, 24, 25, 27

T

Tectaria gemmifera 29
temperate rain forests 18-19
three-in-one fern 35
tissue culture 42
tree ferns 9, 10, 21, 38
tropical rain forests 9, 11, 12-13, 23, 30
tubers 24

U

umbrella fern 13

V

vascular strands 8, 24
vegetable fern 42
vegetative reproduction 29
vine fern 42
Vittaria species 9

W

water clover 11, 16
water ferns 16, 23, 42
water horsetail 17, 31
wetlands 16
wig tree fern 21
Wilson's filmy fern 11

X

xylem 8, 9, 21

A Templar Book